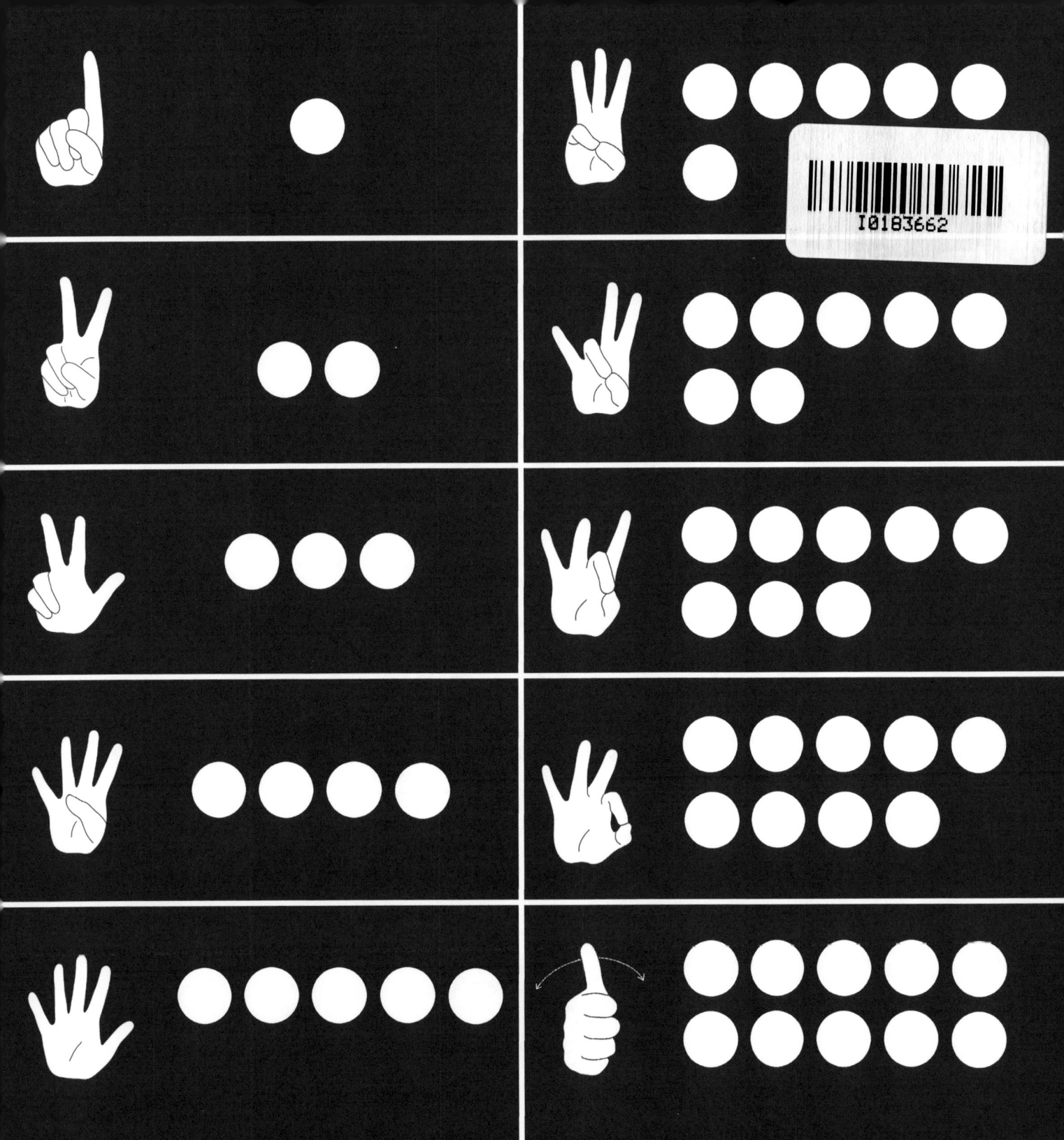

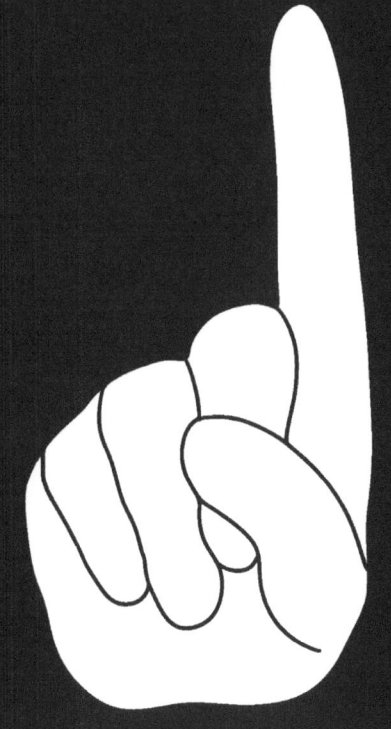

ONE

TWO

THREE

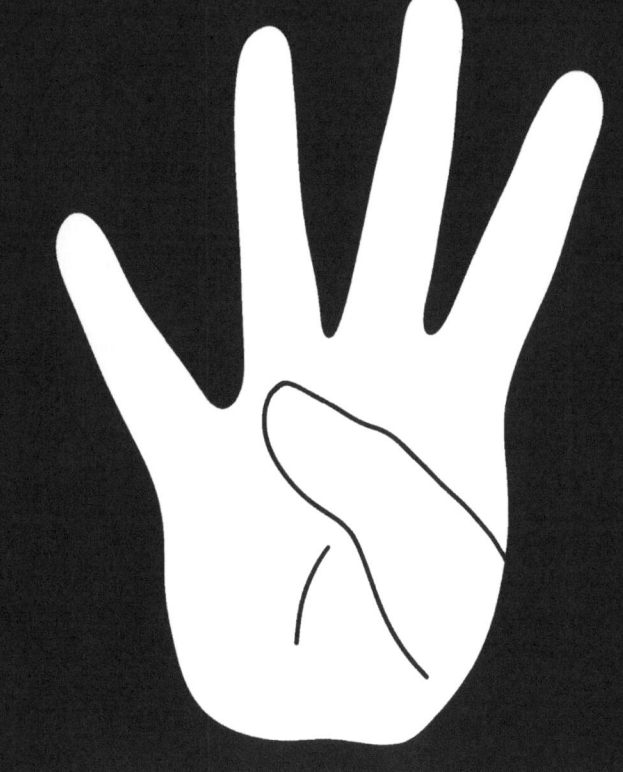

FOUR

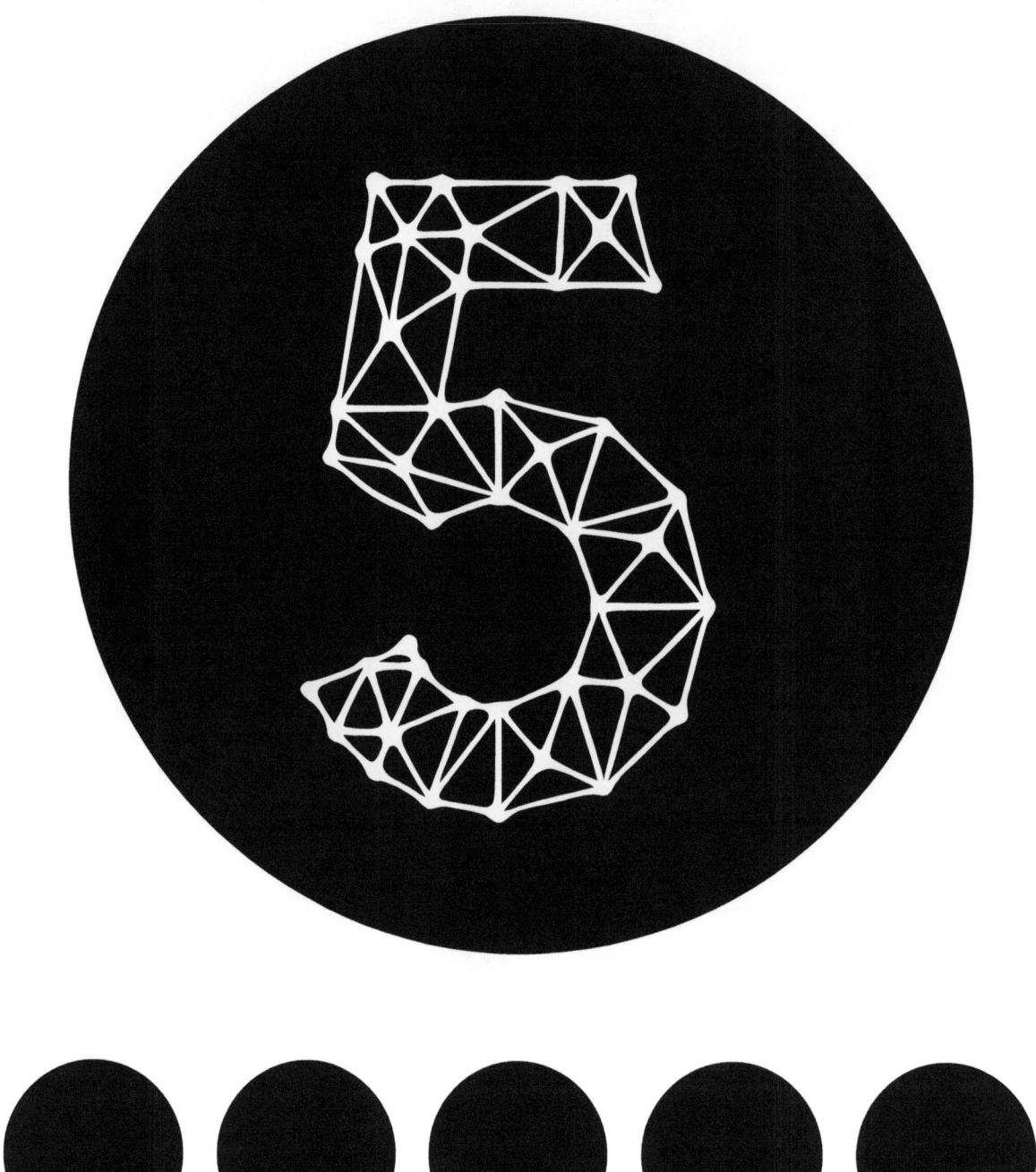

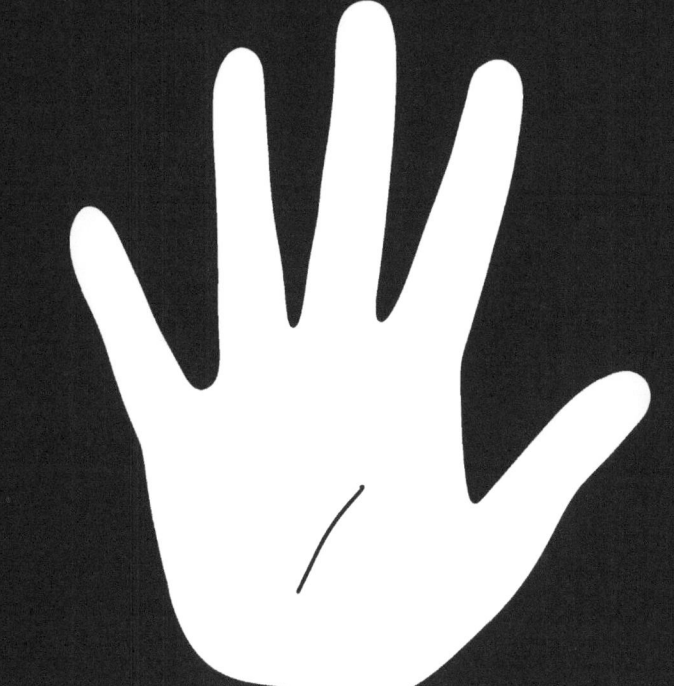

FIVE

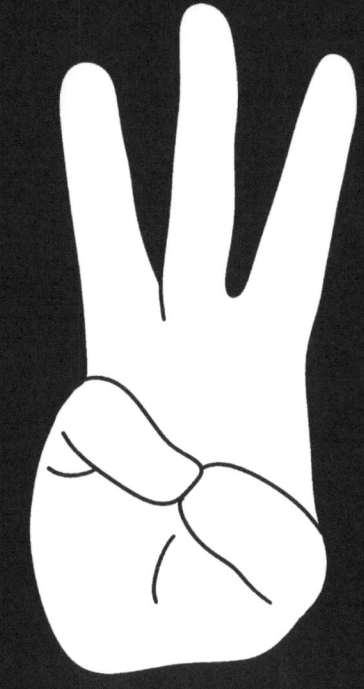

SIX

SEVEN

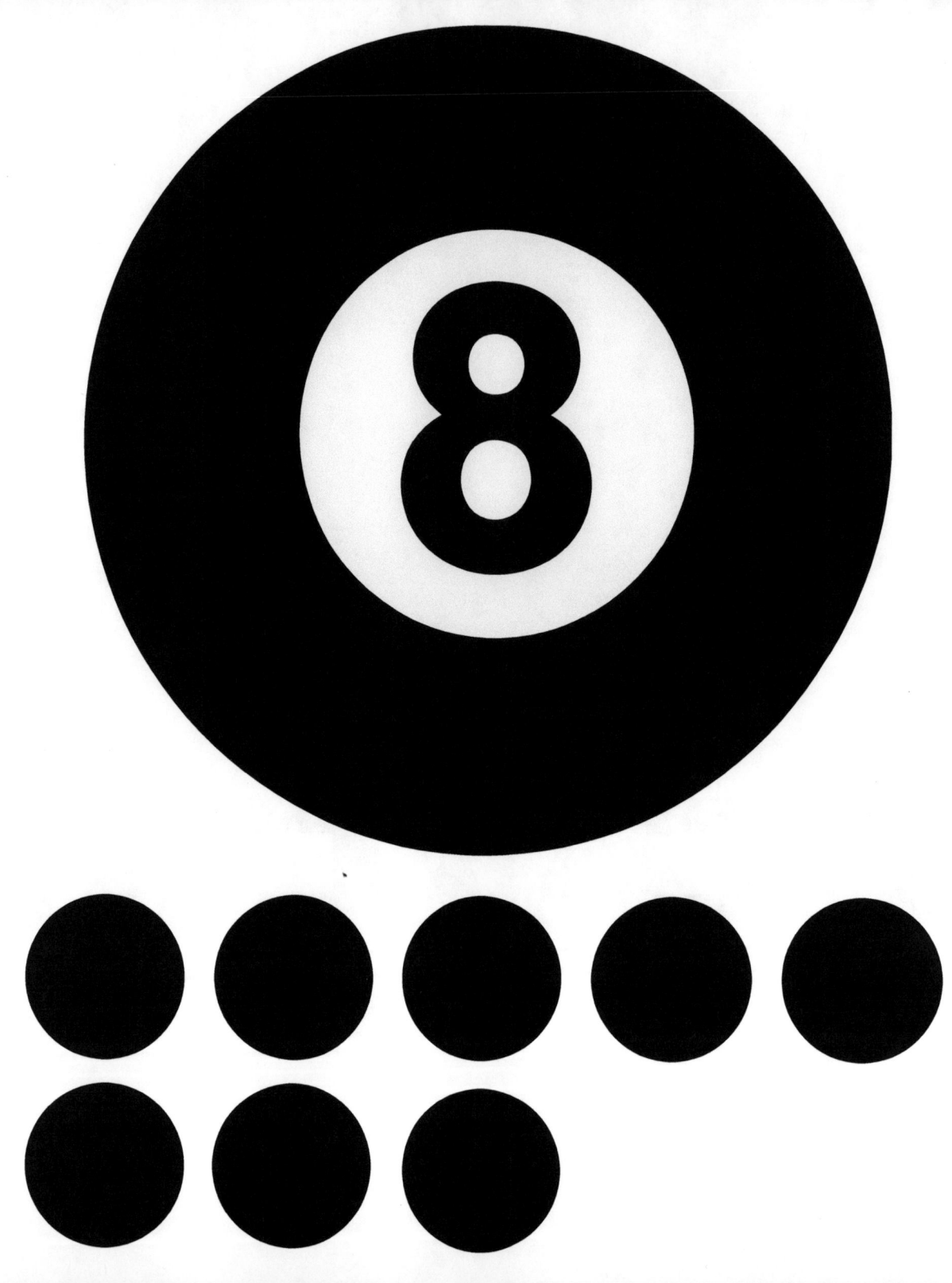

EIGHT

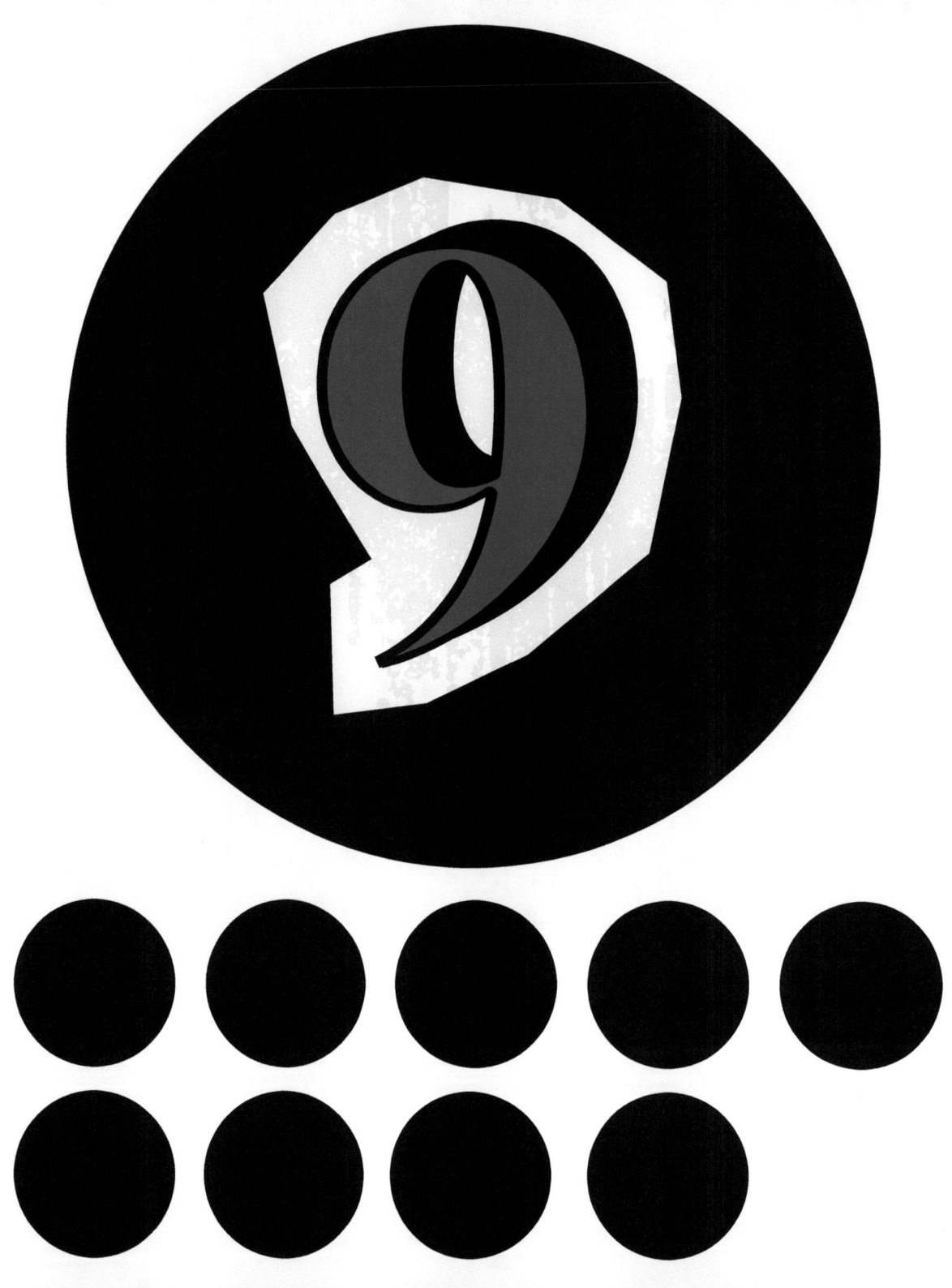

NINE

TEN

	ONE
	TWO
	THREE
	FOUR
	FIVE

	SIX
	SEVEN
	EIGHT
	NINE
	TEN

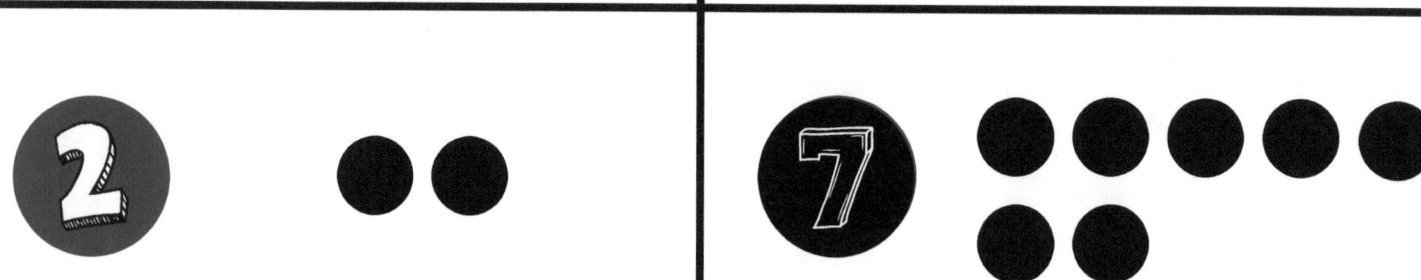
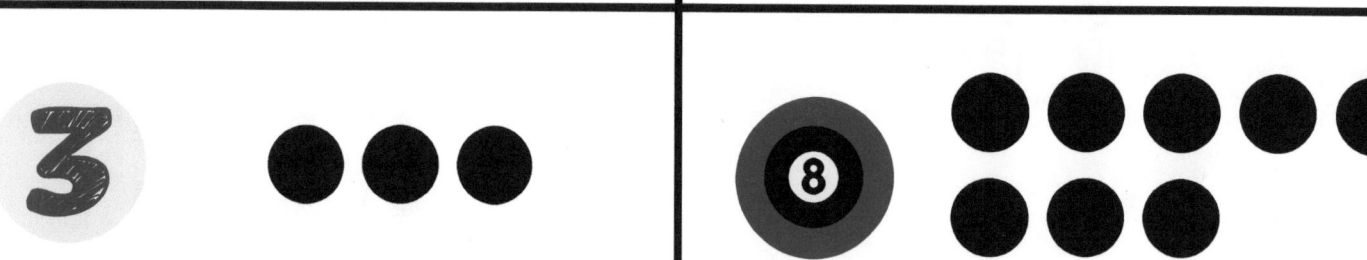

www.ingramcontent.com/pod-product-compliance
Lightning Source LLC
LaVergne TN
LVHW072128070426
835512LV00002B/44